HAL•LEONARD
UKULELE
PLAY-ALONG

AUDIO ACCESS INCLUDED

PLAYBACK+
Speed • Pitch • Balance • Loop

VOL. 37

Play 8 of Your Favorite Songs with Professional Audio Tracks

To access audio visit:
www.halleonard.com/mylibrary

Enter Code
7312-5035-6199-2875

Ukulele by Jay Brian Kummer
Recording production by Chris Kringel

ISBN 978-1-4950-0924-2

7777 W. BLUEMOUND RD. P.O. BOX 13819 MILWAUKEE, WI 53213

Visit Hal Leonard Online at
www.halleonard.com

UKULELE NOTATION LEGEND

THE MUSICAL STAFF shows pitches and rhythms and is divided by bar lines into measures. Pitches are named after the first seven letters of the alphabet.

TABLATURE graphically represents the ukulele fingerboard. Each horizontal line represents a a string, and each number represents a fret.

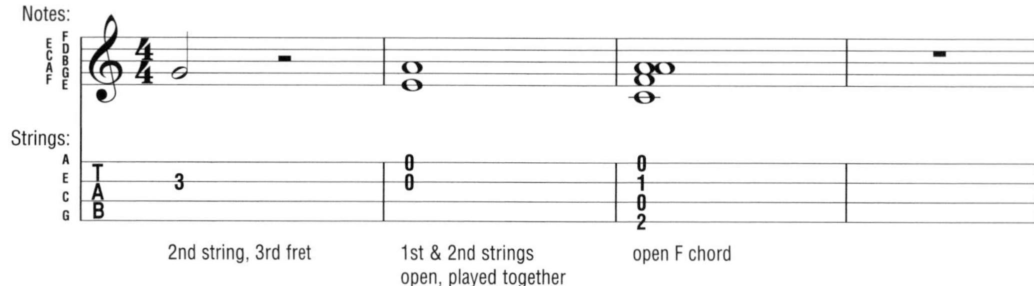

HALF-STEP BEND: Strike the note and bend up 1/2 step.

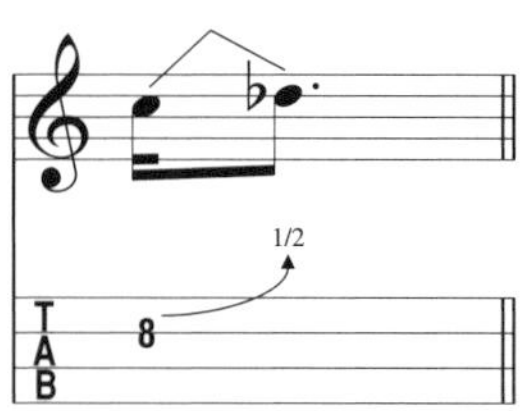

WHOLE-STEP BEND: Strike the note and bend up one step.

GRACE NOTE BEND: Strike the note and immediately bend up as indicated.

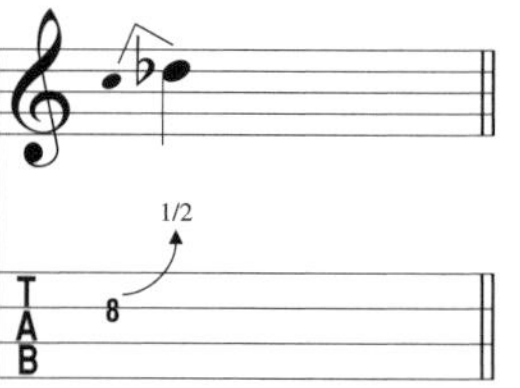

SLIGHT (MICROTONE) BEND: Strike the note and bend up 1/4 step.

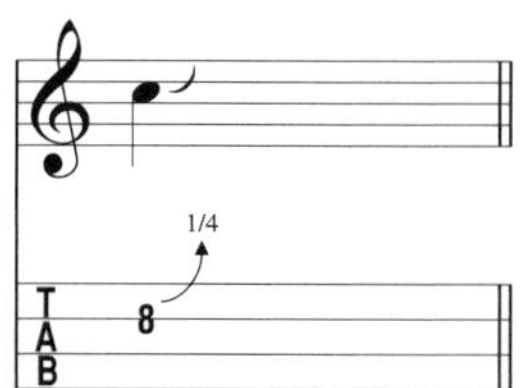

BEND AND RELEASE: Strike the note and bend up as indicated, then release back to the original note. Only the first note is struck.

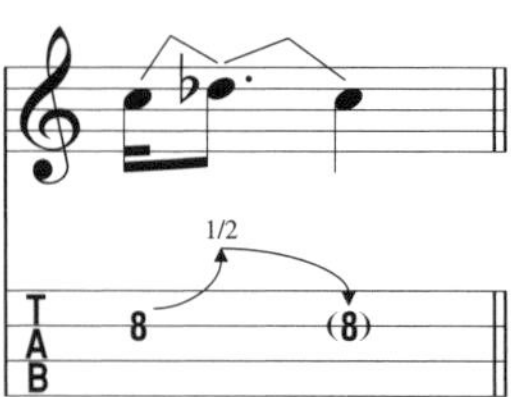

PRE-BEND: Bend the note as indicated, then strike it.

VIBRATO: The string is vibrated by rapidly bending and releasing the note with the fretting hand.

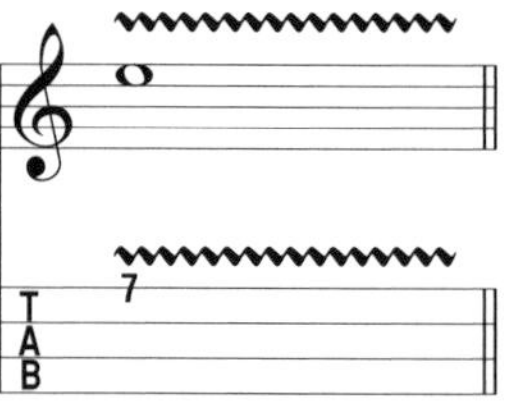

HAMMER-ON: Strike the first (lower) note with one finger, then sound the higher note (on the same string) with another finger by fretting it without picking.

PULL-OFF: Place both fingers on the notes to be sounded. Strike the first note and without picking, pull the finger off to sound the second (lower) note.

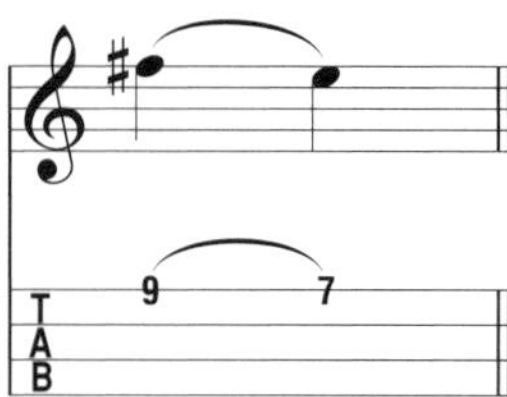

LEGATO SLIDE: Strike the first note and then slide the same fret-hand finger up or down to the second note. The second note is not struck.

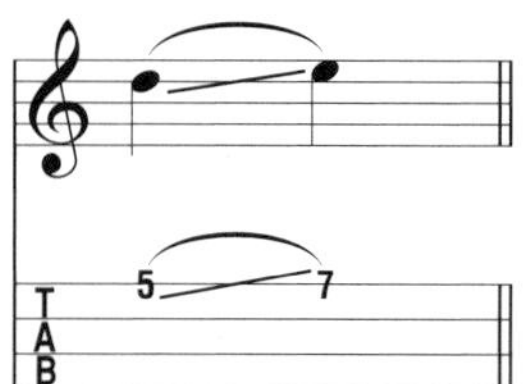

SHIFT SLIDE: Same as legato slide, except the second note is struck.

TRILL: Very rapidly alternate between the notes indicated by continuously hammering on and pulling off.

TREMOLO PICKING: The note is picked as rapidly and continuously as possible.

NOTE: Tablature numbers in parentheses mean:

1. The note is being sustained over a system (note in standard notation is tied), or
2. The note is sustained, but a new articulation (such as a hammer-on, pull-off, slide or vibrato) begins, or
3. The note is a barely audible "ghost" note (note in standard notation is also in parentheses).

Additional Musical Definitions

(accent) • Accentuate note (play it louder)

(staccato) • Play the note short

D.S. al Coda • Go back to the sign (𝄋), then play until the measure marked "***To Coda***," then skip to the section labelled "**Coda**."

D.C. al Fine • Go back to the beginning of the song and play until the measure marked "***Fine***" (end).

N.C. • No chord.

• Repeat measures between signs.

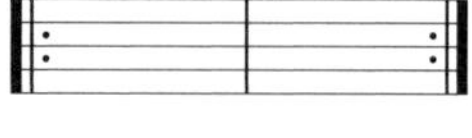

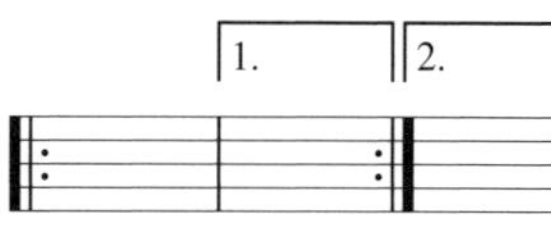

• When a repeated section has different endings, play the first ending only the first time and the second ending only the second time.

CONTENTS

Bésame Mucho

(Kiss Me Much)

Music and Spanish Words by Consuelo Velazquez
English Words by Sunny Skylar

First note

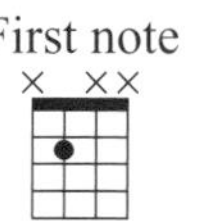

Intro

Moderate Bossa Nova ♩ = 115

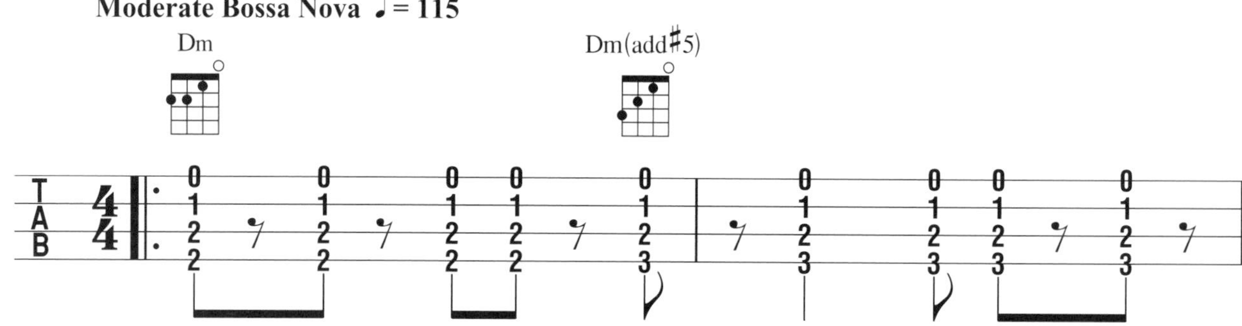

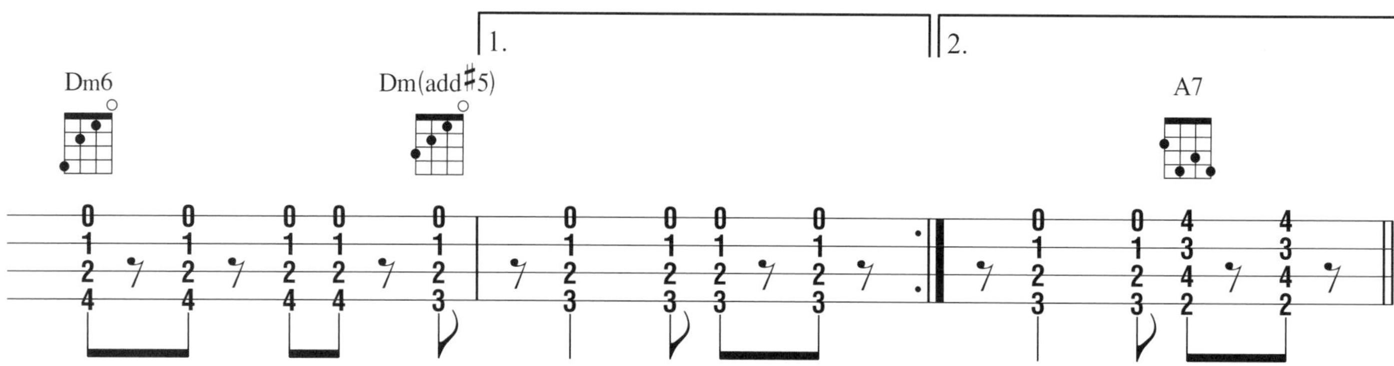

A

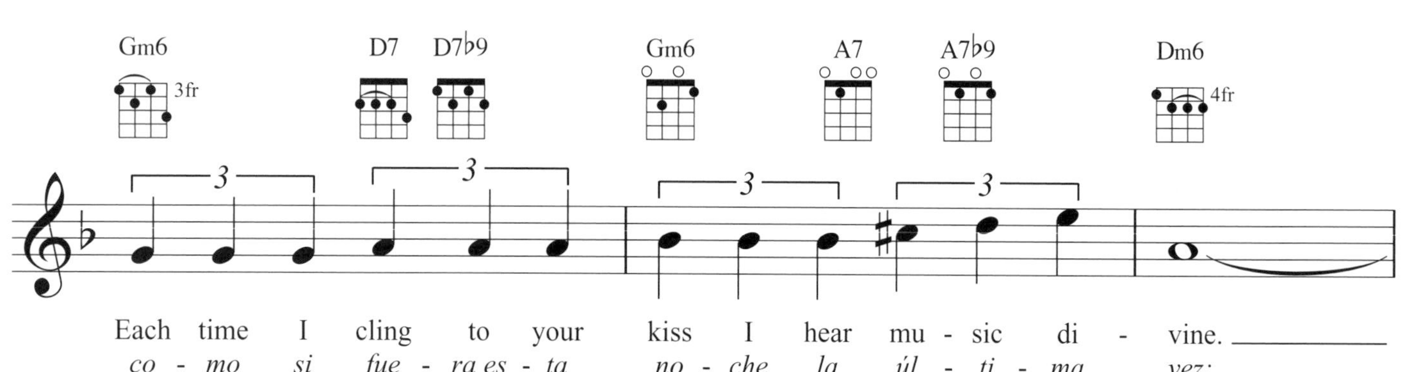

Em7 A7 D7 C D7 D7 D7♭9 Gm6 Gm6
3fr 5fr 5fr 5fr 3fr
Bé - sa - me mu - cho.
bé - sa - me mu - cho,
Gm6 Dm Dm7 B♭7 A7
3fr 5fr 5fr 3fr
Hold me, my dar - ling, and say that you'll al - ways be
que ten - go mie - do per - der - te, per - der - te o - tra
B
Dm6 Dm6 Dm6 Gm6 Dm6
4fr 4fr 3fr 4fr
mine.
vez.
1., 3. This joy is some - thing new, my arms en - fold - ing you,
Quie - ro te - ner - te muy cer - ca, mi - rar - me en tus
2. Solo
A7 Dm6 D7 D7♭9 Gm6
4fr 5fr 5fr 3fr
nev - er knew this thrill be - fore.
o - jos, ver - te jun - to a mí,
Who ev - er thought I'd be
pien - sa que tal vez ma -
Dm6 Dm6 E7 B♭7 A7
3fr
hold - ing you close to me, whis - p'ring, "It's you I a - dore."
fia - na yo ya es - ta - ré le - jos, muy le - jos de ti.

C
Dm6
Dm6
Dm6
Gm6
Gm6
4fr
3fr
2., 6. Dear - est one,
if you should leave me,
Bé - sa - me,
bé - sa - me mu - cho,
4. Solo
Gm6
D7
D7♭9
Gm6
A7
A7♭9
Dm6
Em7
A7
each lit - tle dream would take wing and my life would be through.
co - mo si fue - ra es - ta no - che la úl - ti - ma vez;
D7
C
D7
D7
D7♭9
Gm6
Gm6
Gm6
5fr
Bé - sa - me mu - cho.
bé - sa - me mu - cho,
Dm
Dm7
B♭7
A7
Dm6
Dm6
A7
Play 3 times
Love me for - ev - er and make all my dreams come true.
que ten - go mie - do per - der - te, per - der - te des - pués.
Outro
Dm
Dm7
B♭7
A7
Dm6
Dm6
Dm6
Love me for - ev - er and make all my dreams come true.
Que ten - go mie - do per - der - te, per - der - te des - pués.

Mambo #5

Words and Music by Damaso Perez Prado

B
Bb7
Bb7
3fr
Bb7
6fr
Bb7
3fr
Riff B
End Riff B
Bb7
Bb7
3fr
Bb7
6fr
Bb7
3fr
w/ Riff B
Bb7
N.C.
Bb7
3fr
N.C.
Bb7
6fr
Bb7
10fr
N.C.
C
Bb7
3fr
Bb7
Eb6
5fr
Eb6
*Cue notes 2nd time
Bb7
Bb7
3fr
Bb7
N.C.
6fr
D
Bb7
Eb6
Play 3 times
Si, si, si, yo quie - ro mam - bo, mam - bo!

B♭7
N.C.
B♭7
N.C.
B♭7
N.C.
B♭7
B♭7
3fr
6fr
3fr
E♭6
E♭6
B♭7
B♭7
5fr
3fr
w/ Riff A
E♭6
E♭6
B♭7
N.C.
B♭7
5fr
3fr
E
N.C.
B♭7
N.C.
B♭7
B♭7
B♭7
B♭7
6fr
3fr
6fr
3fr
Riff C
B♭7
B♭7
B♭7
B♭7
3fr
6fr
3fr
End Riff C
w/ Riff C
E♭6
N.C.
E♭6
N.C.
B♭7♯9
5fr
5fr
Play 4 times

A Day in the Life of a Fool

(Manhã de Carnaval)

Words by Carl Sigman
Music by Luiz Bonfa

B
Bm7♭5
E7
Am
4fr
3fr
5fr
Em7♭5
A7
Dm
Dm7
Am7
Fmaj7
Em7
Am9
1.
2.
3.
2., 6. I stop just a - cross from your door but
4. Solo
you're nev - er home an - y - more. So back to my
room and there in the gloom I cry tears of good-
bye. 'Til you come back to me, that's the way it will be ev - 'ry
day in the life of a fool. 5. A 'Til you
come back to me, that's the way it will be ev-'ry day in the life of a fool.

The Gift!
(Recado Bossa Nova)

Music by Djalma Ferreira
Original Lyric by Luiz Antonio
English Lyric by Paul Francis Webster

Bm7♭5
E7
Em7♭5
A7
4fr
4fr
3fr
have flown and we're a - lone. 2., 5. The gift
2.
Cm7
A7
Dm7
5fr
re-mem-ber, dar - ling, nev - er re - fuse the gift of love. For
B
D7
D7
Gm7
Gm
Gm7
5fr
5fr
3fr
love can be a mel - o - dy that ling - ers, or
E7
E7
Am7
A7
4fr
slip like A-pril wine right thru your fing - ers. 3., 6. So kiss
C
Dm7
A7
A7
A7
5fr
5fr
me sweet till our se - cret star

D7
D7
Gm
Gm
Gm7
il - lu - mi - nates the way to Shan - gri - la!
Em7♭5
A7
Dm7
What - ev - er fate may be - fall, all I know is that the gift
To Coda
Cm7
A7
Dm7
Em7♭5
A7
of love is the great - est gift of all.
Solo
Dm7
A7
D7
D7
Gm
Gm
Gm7
Em7♭5
A7
Dm7
1.
Bm7♭5
E7
Em7♭5
A7

2.
Cm7
A7
Dm7
5fr
D7
5fr
D7
Gm7
Gm
Gm7
3fr
E7
4fr
E7
Am7
A7
Dm7
5fr
A7
D7
5fr
D7
Gm7
Gm
Gm7
3fr
Em7♭5
3fr
A7
Dm7
5fr
D.S. al Coda
(take repeat)
Cm7
A7
Dm7
5fr
Em7♭5
3fr
A7
4. No strings
Coda
Outro
Repeat and fade
A7
A7
A7
5fr
Dm7
5fr

The Girl from Ipanema

(Garôta de Ipanema)

Music by Antonio Carlos Jobim
English Words by Norman Gimbel
Original Words by Vinicius De Moraes

First note

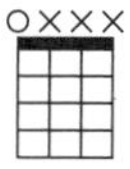

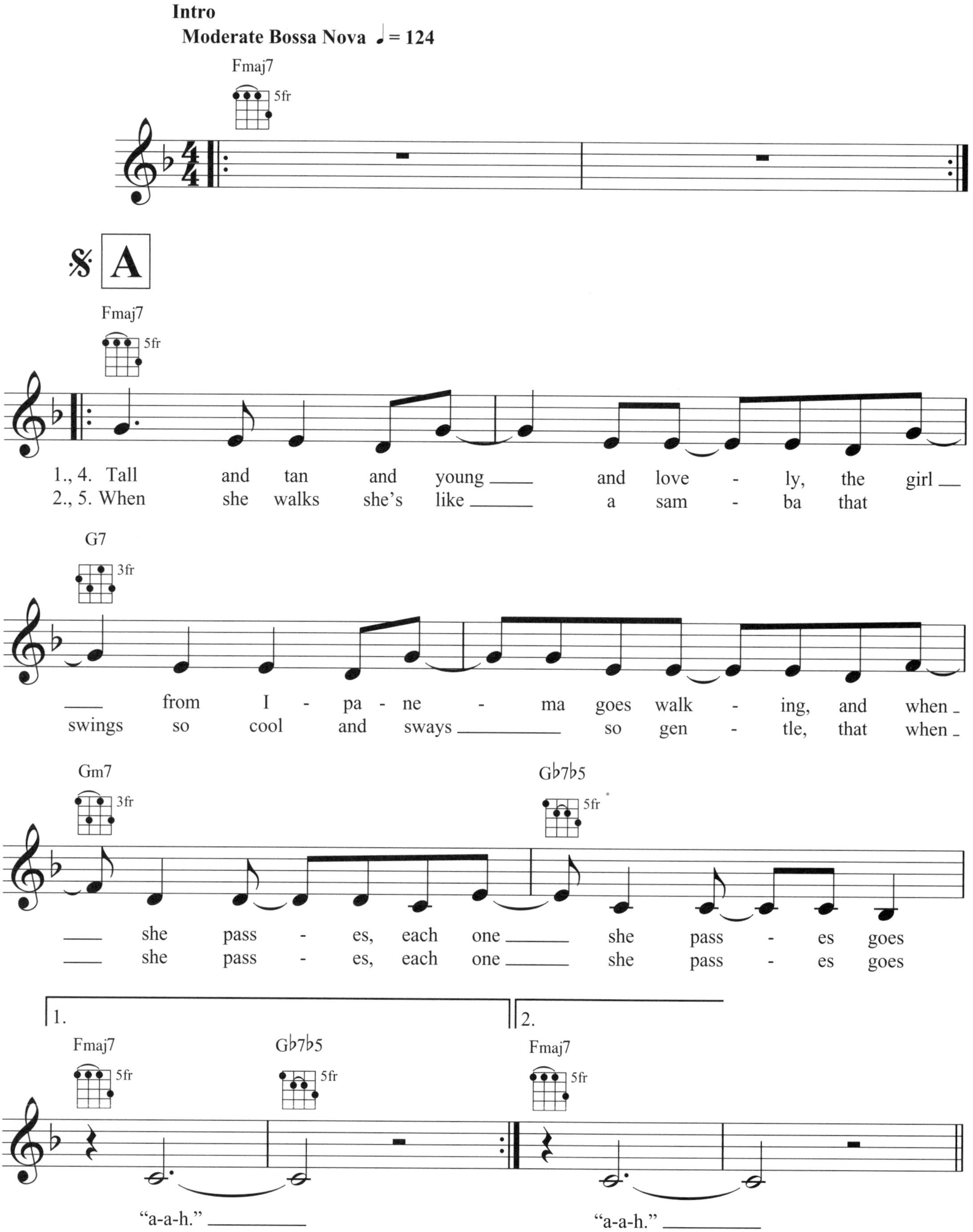

Intro
Moderate Bossa Nova ♩ = 124
Fmaj7
5fr
A
Fmaj7
5fr
1., 4. Tall and tan and young and love - ly, the girl
2., 5. When she walks she's like a sam - ba that
G7
3fr
from I - pa - ne - ma goes walk - ing, and when
swings so cool and sways so gen - tle, that when
Gm7
3fr
Gb7b5
5fr
she pass - es, each one she pass - es goes
she pass - es, each one she pass - es goes
1.
Fmaj7
5fr
Gb7b5
5fr
2.
Fmaj7
5fr
"a-a-h."
"a-a-h."

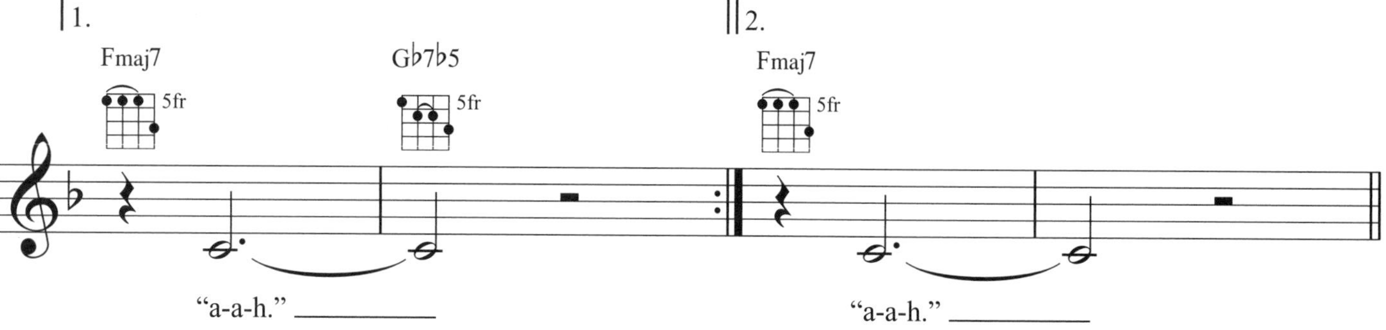

B
G♭maj7
6fr
B9
4fr
Oh, but I watch her so sad - ly. How
F♯m7
D7
5fr
can I tell her I love her? Yes,
Gm7
3fr
E♭9
5fr
I would give my heart glad - ly, but each
Am7
D7♭5
Gm7
day when she walks to the sea, she looks straight a - head not at
C
C7♯11
Fmaj7
5fr
me. 3., 6. Tall and tan and young and love - ly, the girl

G7
3fr
from I - pa - ne - ma goes walk - ing, and when
To Coda
Gm7
3fr
Gb7b5
5fr
Fmaj7
5fr
3
she pass - es I smile, but she does - n't see.
Solo
Gb7b5
5fr
Fmaj7
5fr
G7
3fr
1.
Gm7
3fr
Gb7b5
5fr
Fmaj7
5fr
Gb7b5
5fr
2.
Gbmaj7
6fr
B9
4fr
F#m7
D7
5fr

Gm7
3fr
E♭9
5fr
Am7
D7♭5
Gm7
C7♯11
Fmaj7
5fr
G7
3fr
D.S. al Coda
(take repeat)
Gm7
3fr
G♭7♭5
5fr
Fmaj7
5fr
G♭7♭5
5fr
Coda
G♭7♭5
5fr
Fmaj7
5fr
G♭7♭5
5fr
3
3
She just does - n't see.
No, she does - n't
Fmaj7
5fr
G♭7♭5
5fr
Fmaj7
5fr
see.

One Note Samba
(Samba de Uma Nota So)

Original Lyrics by Newton Mendonça
English Lyrics by Antonio Carlos Jobim
Music by Antonio Carlos Jobim

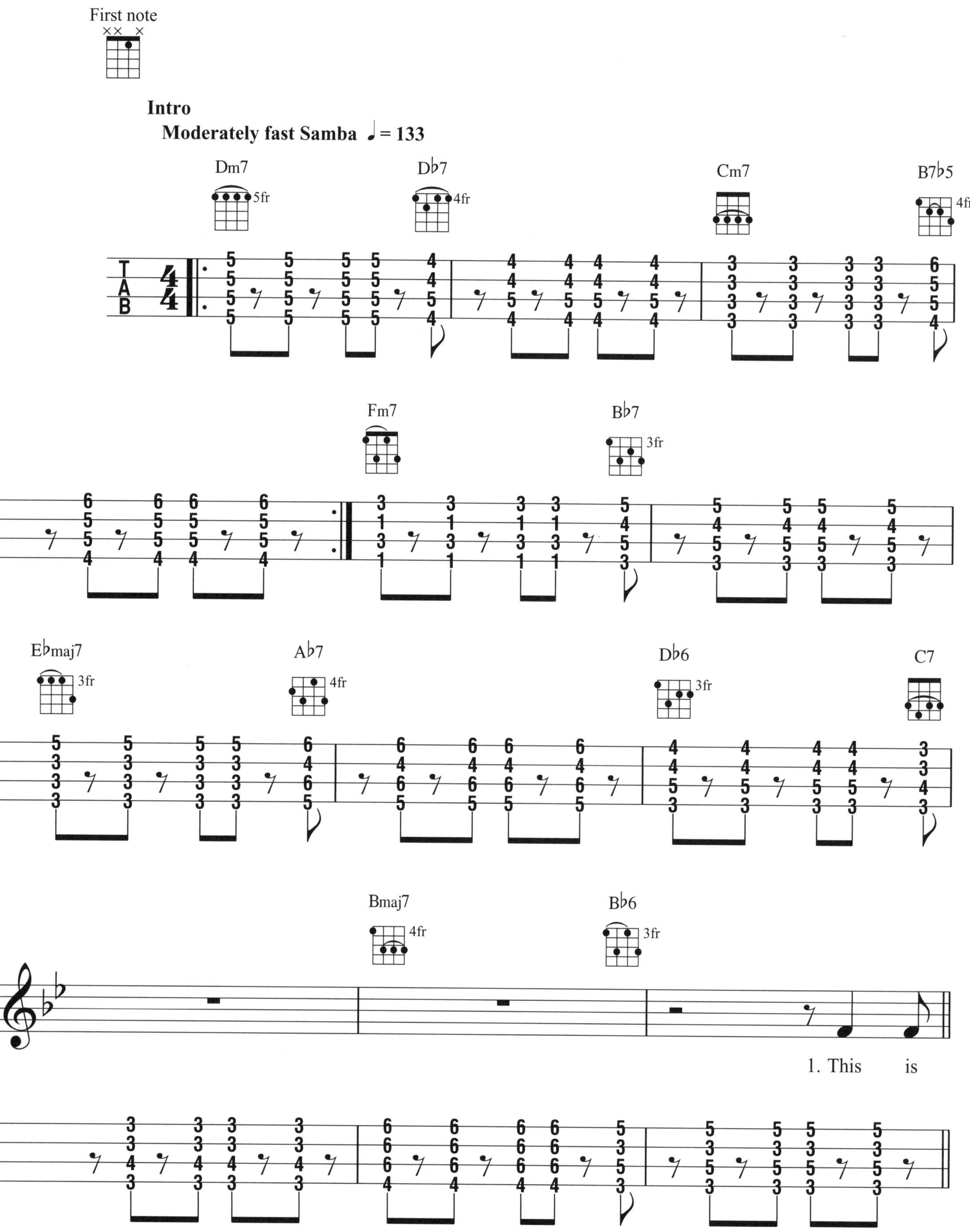

A
Dm7
5fr
D♭7
4fr
Cm7
cont. sim.
(5.) just a lit - tle sam - ba built up - on a sin - gle note.
3. Solo
B7♭5
4fr
Dm7
5fr
D♭7
6fr
Oth - er notes are bound to fol - low, but the
Cm7
5fr
B7♭5
4fr
Fm7
root is still that note. Now the new one is the con -
B♭7
3fr
E♭maj7
3fr
A♭7
4fr
- se - quence of the one we've just been through, as I'm
Dm7
5fr
D♭7
4fr
Cm7
B7♭5
4fr
bound to be the un - a - void - a - ble con - se - quence of you.

B
B♭6
3fr
E♭m7
6fr
1., 3. There's so man - y peo - ple who can
2. Solo
A♭7
4fr
D♭maj7
talk and talk and talk and just say noth - ing, or near - ly noth - ing.
D♭m7
G♭7
I have used up all the scale I know and at the end I've come to
C
Bmaj7
4fr
Cm7♭5
5fr
B7♭5
4fr
Dm7
5fr
noth - ing, or near - ly noth - ing. 2., 6. So I come back to my first
4. Solo
D♭7
4fr
Cm7
B7♭5
4fr
note, as I must come back to you. I will

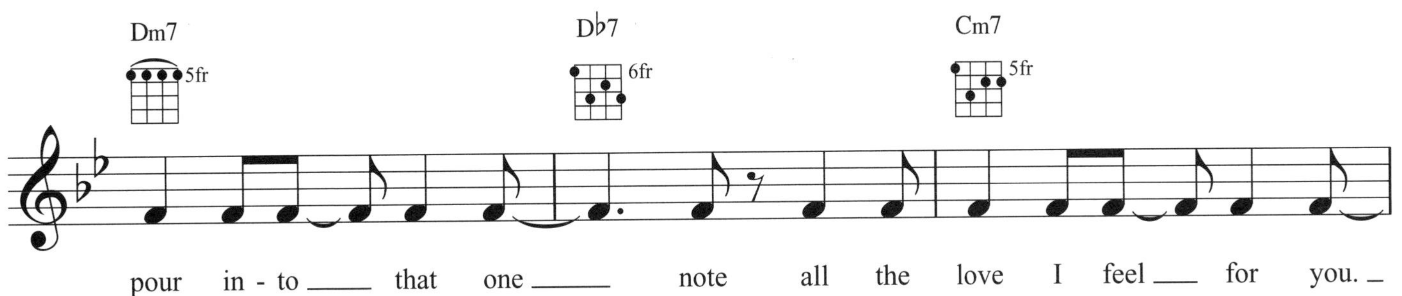
Dm7
5fr
Db7
6fr
Cm7
5fr
pour in - to that one note all the love I feel for you.

B7b5
4fr
Fm7
Bb7
3fr
An - y - one who wants the whole show re, mi,

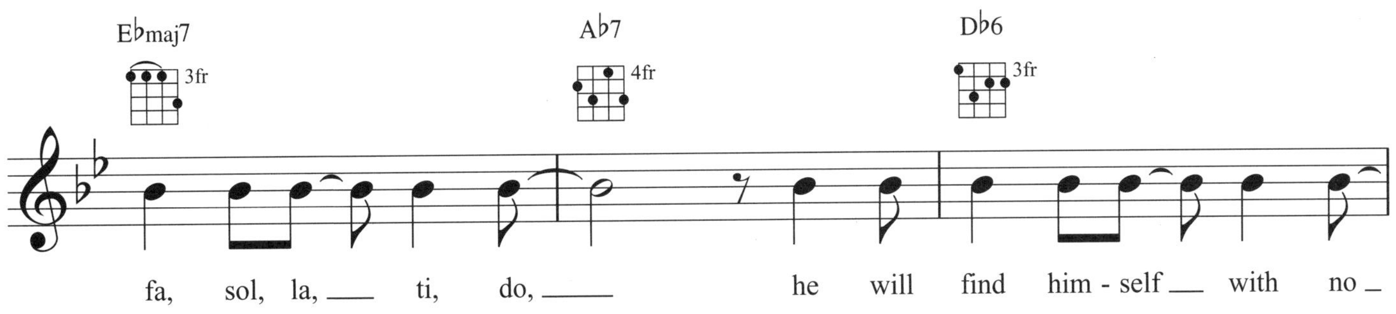
Ebmaj7
3fr
Ab7
4fr
Db6
3fr
fa, sol, la, ti, do, he will find him - self with no

1.
C7
Bmaj7
4fr
Bb6
3fr
F7#5
show. Bet - ter play the note you know.

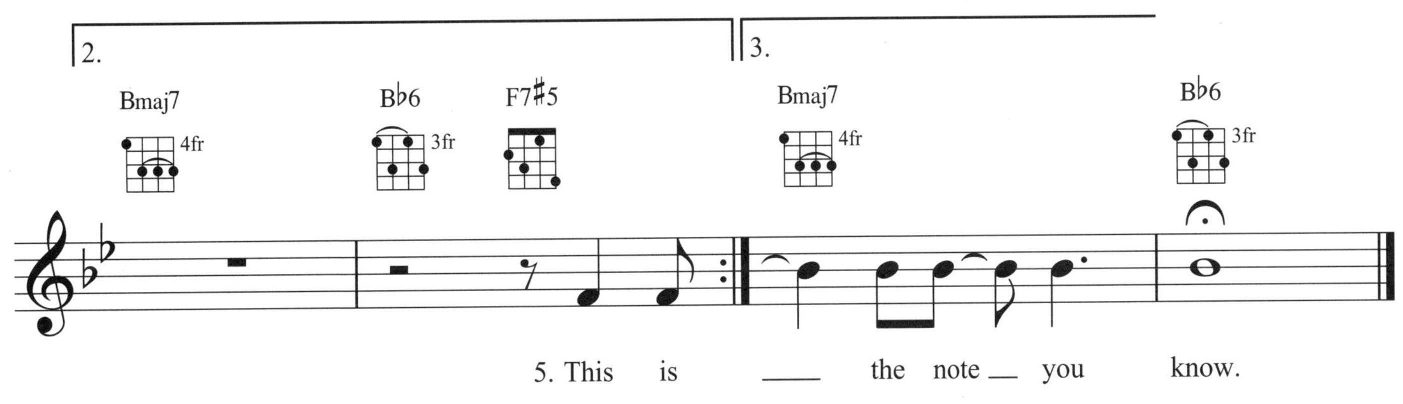
2.
3.
Bmaj7
4fr
Bb6
3fr
F7#5
Bmaj7
4fr
Bb6
3fr
5. This is the note you know.

Quiet Nights of Quiet Stars

(Corcovado)

English Words by Gene Lees
Original Words and Music by Antonio Carlos Jobim

First note

Intro
Moderately fast Bossa Nova ♩ = 140

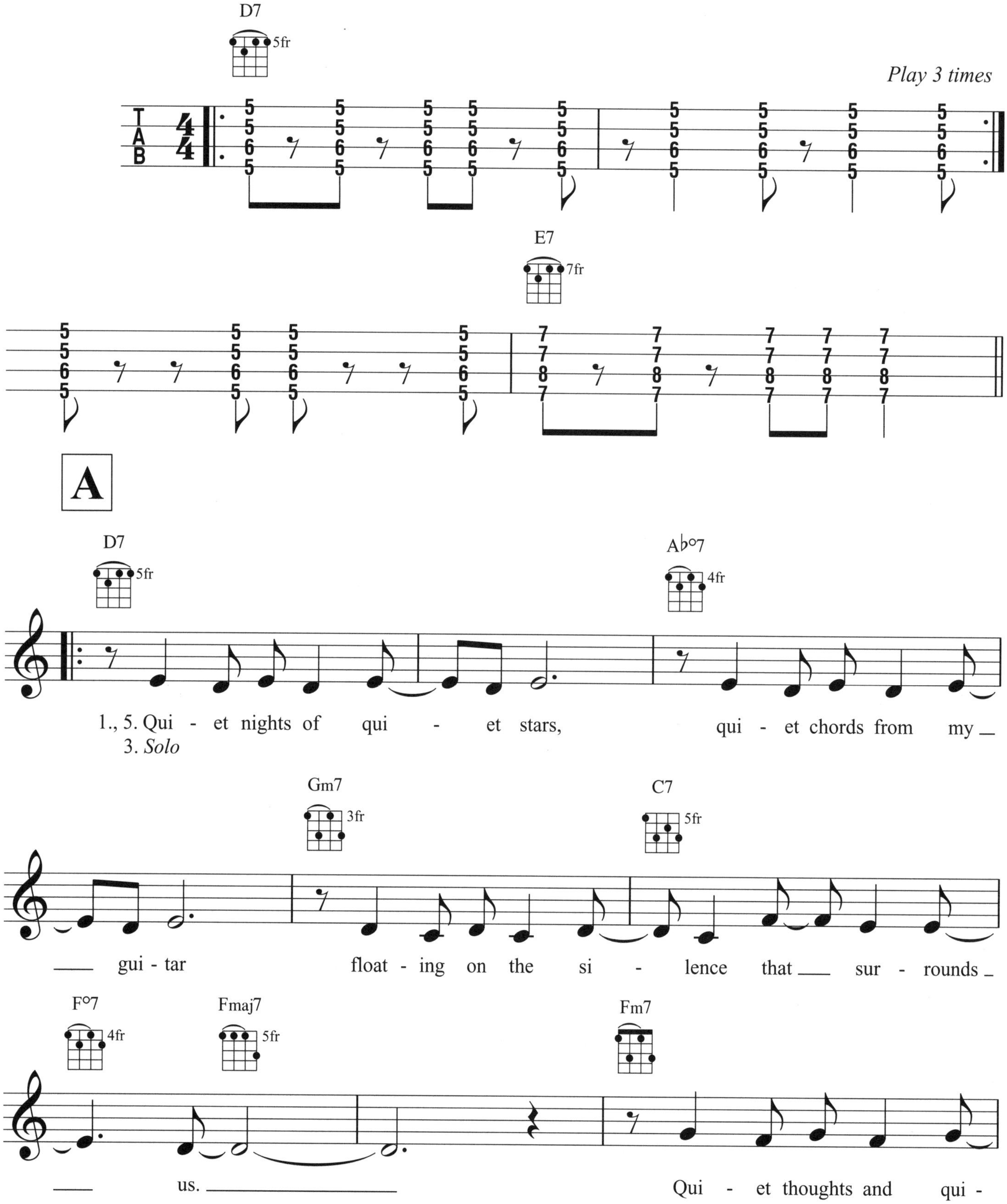

D7 5fr

Play 3 times

E7 7fr

A

D7 5fr   A♭°7 4fr

1., 5. Qui - et nights of qui - et stars, qui - et chords from my
3. *Solo*

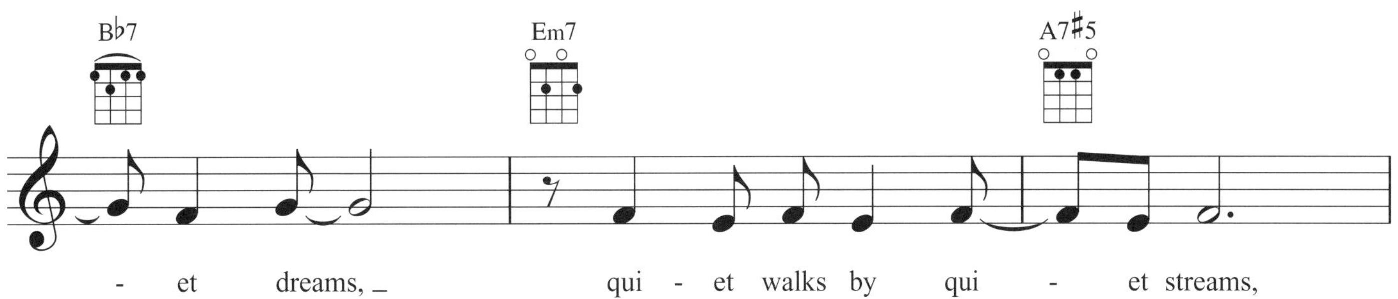
B♭7
Em7
A7♯5
- et dreams, quiet walks by qui - et streams,
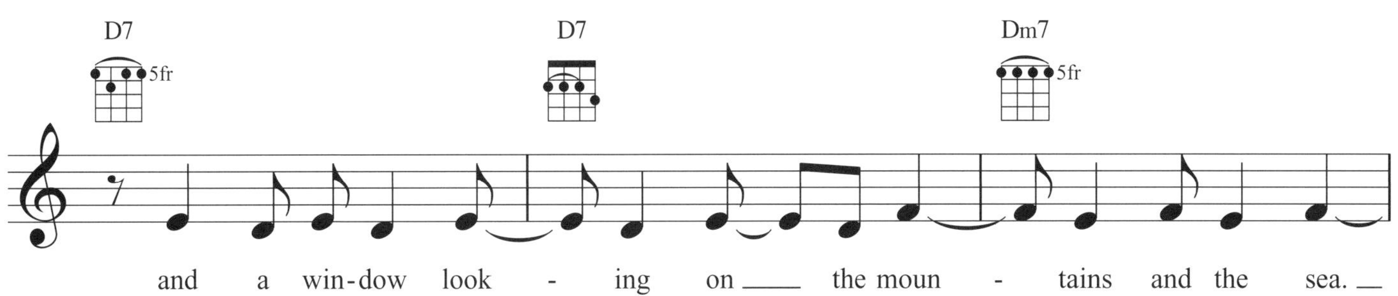
D7
5fr
D7
Dm7
5fr
and a win-dow look - ing on the moun - tains and the sea.

B
A♭°7
4fr
D7
5fr
How love - ly! 2., 6. This is where I want to be.
4. Solo

A♭°7
4fr
Gm7
3fr
3
Here, with you so close to me, un - til the fi - nal
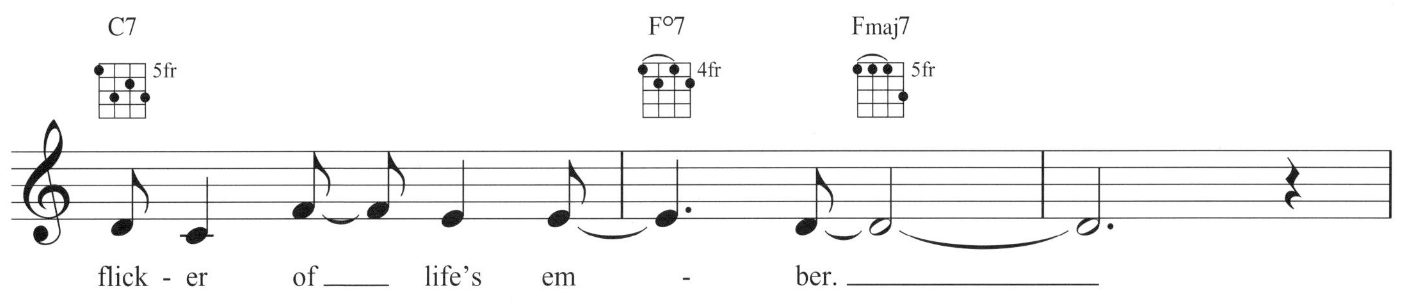
C7
5fr
F°7
4fr
Fmaj7
5fr
flick - er of life's em - ber.

Fm7
B♭7♭5
Em7
I, who was lost and lone - ly,
be - liev - ing life was

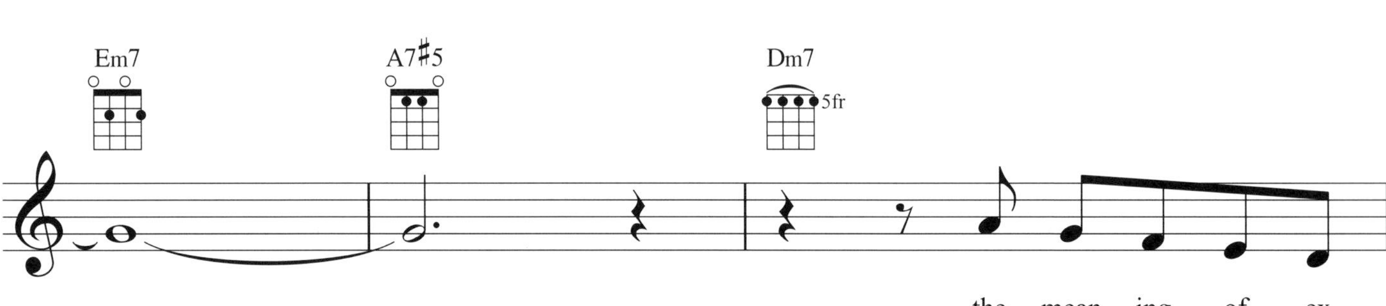
Am7
Dm7
G7
on - ly
a bit - ter, trag - ic joke, have found with you

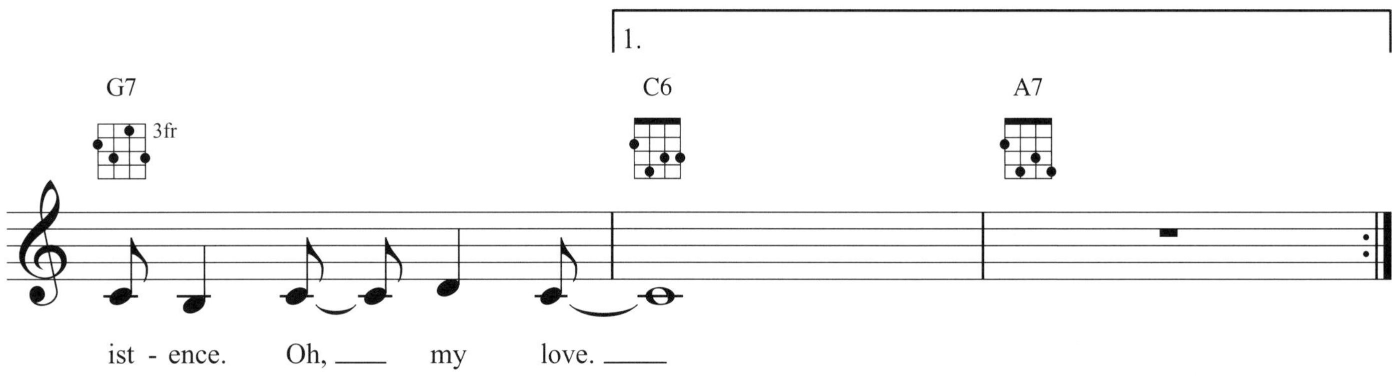
Em7
A7♯5
Dm7
5fr
the mean - ing of ex -

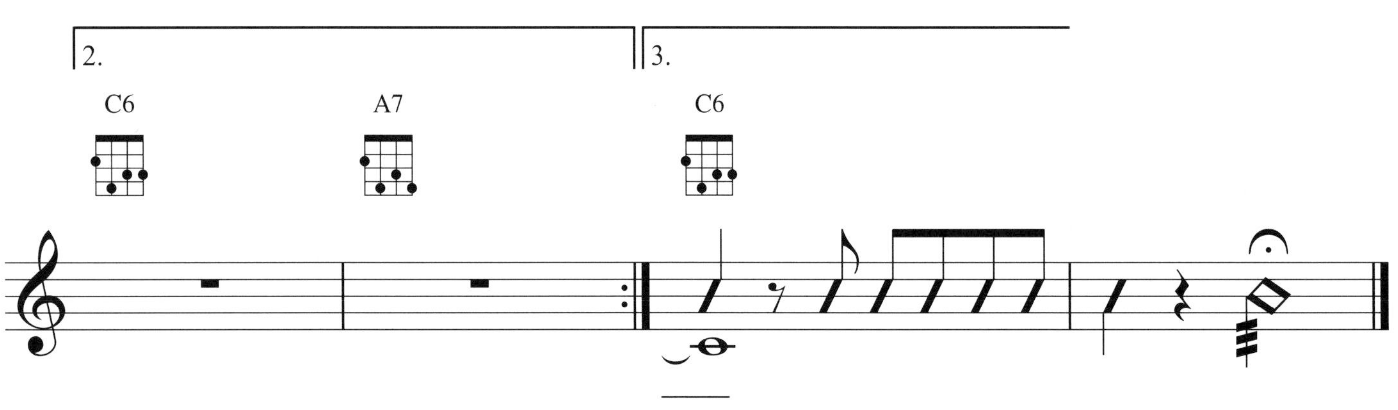
1.
G7
3fr
C6
A7
ist - ence. Oh, my love.
2.
C6
A7
3.
C6

Wave

Words and Music by Antonio Carlos Jobim

1.
B♭7
A7♯5
Dm7
G7
Dm7
G7
two can dream a dream to - geth - er.
2., 8. You can't de -
2.
B
Dm7
G7
Gm7
3fr
C7
3
1., 3. When I saw you first the time was
2. Solo
Am7
Am7
5fr
Fm7
4fr
half past three. When your eyes met
B♭7
3fr
Gm7
A7
A7♭9
mine, it was e - ter - ni - ty.
3., 9. By now we
C
Dmaj7
B♭°7
3fr
Am7
know the wave is on its way to be.
6. Solo

D7
D7♭9
Gmaj7
Gm6
Just catch the wave don't be a - fraid of lov - ing me.
F♯7
F♯7♯5
2fr
B9
B7
B7♭9
Bm7
E7
The fun - da - men - tal lone - li - ness goes when - ev - er
To Coda 1
To Coda 2
D.S. al Coda 1
(take repeat)
B♭7
A7♯5
Dm7
G7
Dm7
G7
two can dream a dream to - geth - er.
Coda 1
D.S. al Coda 2
(take repeat)
Coda 2
Dm7
G7
Dm7
G7
7. So close your
Dm7
G7
Dm7
G7
- er.
Outro
Dm7
G7
Dm7
G7
Dm7
5fr

HAL•LEONARD®

UKULELE PLAY-ALONG

AUDIO ACCESS INCLUDED

Now you can play your favorite songs on your uke with great-sounding backing tracks to help you sound like a bona fide pro! The audio also features playback tools so you can adjust the tempo without changing the pitch and loop challenging parts.

1. POP HITS
00701451 Book/CD Pack...............$15.99

2. UKE CLASSICS
00701452 Book/CD Pack...............$14.99

3. HAWAIIAN FAVORITES
00701453 Book/Online Audio..........$12.99

4. CHILDREN'S SONGS
00701454 Book/CD Pack...............$12.99

5. CHRISTMAS SONGS
00701696 Book/CD Pack...............$12.99

6. LENNON & MCCARTNEY
00701723 Book/Online Audio..........$12.99

7. DISNEY FAVORITES
00701724 Book/Online Audio..........$12.99

8. CHART HITS
00701745 Book/CD Pack...............$15.99

9. THE SOUND OF MUSIC
00701784 Book/CD Pack...............$12.99

10. MOTOWN
00701964 Book/CD Pack...............$12.99

11. CHRISTMAS STRUMMING
00702458 Book/CD Pack...............$12.99

12. BLUEGRASS FAVORITES
00702584 Book/CD Pack...............$12.99

13. UKULELE SONGS
00702599 Book/CD Pack...............$12.99

Prices, contents, and availability subject to change without notice.

14. JOHNNY CASH
00702615 Book/CD Pack...............$15.99

15. COUNTRY CLASSICS
00702834 Book/CD Pack...............$12.99

16. STANDARDS
00702835 Book/CD Pack...............$12.99

17. POP STANDARDS
00702836 Book/CD Pack...............$12.99

18. IRISH SONGS
00703086 Book/Online Audio..........$12.99

19. BLUES STANDARDS
00703087 Book/CD Pack...............$12.99

20. FOLK POP ROCK
00703088 Book/CD Pack...............$12.99

21. HAWAIIAN CLASSICS
00703097 Book/CD Pack...............$12.99

22. ISLAND SONGS
00703098 Book/CD Pack...............$12.99

23. TAYLOR SWIFT – 2ND EDITION
00221966 Book/Online Audio..........$16.99

24. WINTER WONDERLAND
00101871 Book/CD Pack...............$12.99

25. GREEN DAY
00110398 Book/CD Pack...............$14.99

www.halleonard.com

26. BOB MARLEY
00110399 Book/Online Audio..........$14.99

27. TIN PAN ALLEY
00116358 Book/CD Pack...............$12.99

28. STEVIE WONDER
00116736 Book/CD Pack...............$14.99

29. OVER THE RAINBOW & OTHER FAVORITES
00117076 Book/CD Pack...............$14.99

30. ACOUSTIC SONGS
00122336 Book/CD Pack...............$14.99

31. JASON MRAZ
00124166 Book/CD Pack...............$14.99

32. TOP DOWNLOADS
00127507 Book/CD Pack...............$14.99

33. CLASSICAL THEMES
00127892 Book/Online Audio..........$14.99

34. CHRISTMAS HITS
00128602 Book/CD Pack...............$14.99

35. SONGS FOR BEGINNERS
00129009 Book/Online Audio..........$14.99

36. ELVIS PRESLEY HAWAII
00138199 Book/Online Audio..........$14.99

39. GYPSY JAZZ
00146559 Book/Online Audio..........$14.99

40. TODAY'S HITS
00160845 Book/Online Audio..........$14.99

0817

Ride the Ukulele Wave!

The Beach Boys for Ukulele

This folio features 20 favorites, including: Barbara Ann • Be True to Your School • California Girls • Fun, Fun, Fun • God Only Knows • Good Vibrations • Help Me Rhonda • I Get Around • In My Room • Kokomo • Little Deuce Coupe • Sloop John B • Surfin' U.S.A. • Wouldn't It Be Nice • and more!

00701726 . . . .$14.99

The Beatles for Ukulele

Ukulele players can strum, sing and pick along with 20 Beatles classics! Includes: All You Need Is Love • Eight Days a Week • Good Day Sunshine • Here, There and Everywhere • Let It Be • Love Me Do • Penny Lane • Yesterday • and more.

00700154 . . . .$16.99

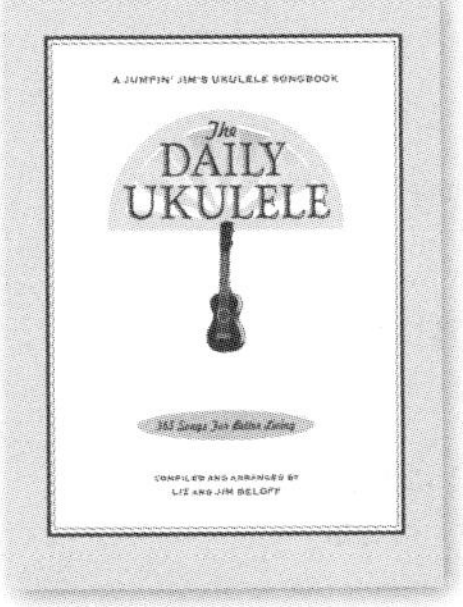

The Daily Ukulele

compiled and arranged by

Liz and Jim Beloff

Strum a different song everyday with easy arrangements of 365 of your favorite songs in one big songbook! Includes favorites by the Beatles, Beach Boys, and Bob Dylan, folk songs, pop songs, kids' songs, Christmas carols, and Broadway and Hollywood tunes, all with a spiral binding for ease of use.

00240356 . . . .$39.99

The Daily Ukulele – Leap Year Edition

366 More Songs for Better Living

compiled and arranged by

Liz and Jim Beloff

An amazing second volume with 366 MORE songs for you to master each day of a leap year! Includes: Ain't No Sunshine • Calendar Girl • I Got You Babe • Lean on Me • Moondance • and many, many more.

00240681 . . . .$39.99

Disney Songs for Ukulele

20 great Disney classics arranged for all uke players, including: Beauty and the Beast • Bibbidi-Bobbidi-Boo (The Magic Song) • Can You Feel the Love Tonight • Chim Chim Cher-ee • Heigh-Ho • It's a Small World • Some Day My Prince Will Come • We're All in This Together • When You Wish upon a Star • and more.

00701708 . . . .$14.99

First 50 Songs You Should Play on Ukulele

An amazing collection of 50 accessible, must-know favorites: Edelweiss • Hey, Soul Sister • I Walk the Line • I'm Yours • Imagine • Over the Rainbow • Peaceful Easy Feeling • The Rainbow Connection • Riptide • and many more.

00149250 . . . .$14.99

Folk Songs for Ukulele

A great collection to take along to the campfire! 60 folk songs, including: Amazing Grace • Buffalo Gals • Camptown Races • For He's a Jolly Good Fellow • Good Night Ladies • Home on the Range • I've Been Working on the Railroad • Kumbaya • My Bonnie Lies over the Ocean • On Top of Old Smoky • Scarborough Fair • Swing Low, Sweet Chariot • Take Me Out to the Ball Game • Yankee Doodle • and more.

00696068 . . . .$12.99

Hawaiian Songs for Ukulele

Over thirty songs from the state that made the ukulele famous, including: Beyond the Rainbow • Hanalei Moon • Ka-lu-a • Lovely Hula Girl • Mele Kalikimaka • One More Aloha • Sea Breeze • Tiny Bubbles • Waikiki • and more.

00696065 . . . .$10.99

Jack Johnson – Strum & Sing

Cherry Lane Music

Strum along with 41 Jack Johnson songs using this top-notch collection of chords and lyrics just for the uke! Includes: Better Together • Bubble Toes • Cocoon • Do You Remember • Flake • Fortunate Fool • Good People • Holes to Heaven • Taylor • Tomorrow Morning • and more.

02501702 . . . .$17.99

Elvis Presley for Ukulele

arr. Jim Beloff

20 classic hits from The King: All Shook Up • Blue Hawaii • Blue Suede Shoes • Can't Help Falling in Love • Don't • Heartbreak Hotel • Hound Dog • Jailhouse Rock • Love Me • Love Me Tender • Return to Sender • Suspicious Minds • Teddy Bear • and more.

00701004 . . . .$15.99

Jake Shimabukuro – Peace Love Ukulele

Deemed "the Hendrix of the ukulele," Hawaii native Jake Shimabukuro is a uke virtuoso. Our songbook features note-for-note transcriptions with ukulele tablature of Jake's masterful playing on all the CD tracks: Bohemian Rhapsody • Boy Meets Girl • Bring Your Adz • Hallelujah • Pianoforte 2010 • Variation on a Dance 2010 • and more, plus two bonus selections!

00702516 . . . .$19.99

Worship Songs for Ukulele

25 worship songs: Amazing Grace (My Chains are Gone) • Blessed Be Your Name • Enough • God of Wonders • Holy Is the Lord • How Great Is Our God • In Christ Alone • Love the Lord • Mighty to Save • Sing to the King • Step by Step • We Fall Down • and more.

00702546 . . . .$14.99

UKULELE ENSEMBLE SERIES

The songs in these collections are playable by any combination of ukuleles (soprano, concert, tenor or baritone). Each arrangement features the melody, a harmony part, and a "bass" line. Chord symbols are also provided if you wish to add a rhythm part. For groups with more than three or four ukuleles, the parts may be doubled.

CHRISTMAS CAROLS

Early Intermediate Level

Away in a Manger • Carol of the Bells • Deck the Hall • The First Noel • God Rest Ye Merry, Gentlemen • Hark! the Herald Angels Sing • It Came Upon the Midnight Clear • Jingle Bells • Joy to the World • O Christmas Tree • O Come, All Ye Faithful • O Holy Night • O Little Town of Bethlehem • Silent Night • Up on the Housetop.

00129248 .... $9.99

CHRISTMAS SONGS

Early Intermediate Level

The Chipmunk Song • The Christmas Song (Chestnuts Roasting on an Open Fire) • Do You Hear What I Hear • Feliz Navidad • Frosty the Snow Man • Have Yourself a Merry Little Christmas • Here Comes Santa Claus (Right Down Santa Claus Lane) • A Holly Jolly Christmas • (There's No Place Like) Home for the Holidays • Jingle Bell Rock • The Little Drummer Boy • Merry Christmas, Darling • The Most Wonderful Time of the Year • Silver Bells • White Christmas.

00129247 .... $9.99

CLASSIC ROCK

Mid-Intermediate Level

Aqualung • Behind Blue Eyes • Born to Be Wild • Crazy Train • Fly Like an Eagle • Free Bird • Hey Jude • Low Rider • Moondance • Oye Como Va • Proud Mary • (I Can't Get No) Satisfaction • Smoke on the Water • Summertime Blues • Sunshine of Your Love.

00103904 .... $9.99

HAWAIIAN SONGS

Mid-Intermediate Level

Aloha Oe • Beyond the Rainbow • Harbor Lights • Hawaiian War Chant (Ta-Hu-Wa-Hu-Wai) • The Hawaiian Wedding Song (Ke Kali Nei Au) • Ka-lu-a • Lovely Hula Hands • Mele Kalikimaka • The Moon of Manakoora • One Paddle, Two Paddle • Pearly Shells (Pupu 'O 'Ewa) • Red Sails in the Sunset • Sleepy Lagoon • Song of the Islands • Tiny Bubbles.

00119254 .... $9.99

THE NUTCRACKER

Late Intermediate Level

Arabian Dance ("Coffee") • Chinese Dance ("Tea") • Dance of the Reed-Flutes • Dance of the Sugar Plum Fairy • March • Overture • Russian Dance ("Trepak") • Waltz of the Flowers.

00119908 .... $9.99

ROCK INSTRUMENTALS

Late Intermediate Level

Beck's Bolero • Cissy Strut • Europa (Earth's Cry Heaven's Smile) • Frankenstein • Green Onions • Jessica • Misirlou • Perfidia • Pick Up the Pieces • Pipeline • Rebel 'Rouser • Sleepwalk • Tequila • Walk Don't Run • Wipe Out.

00103909 .... $9.99

STANDARDS & GEMS

Mid-Intermediate Level

Autumn Leaves • Cheek to Cheek • Easy to Love • Fly Me to the Moon • I Only Have Eyes for You • It Had to Be You • Laura • Mack the Knife • My Funny Valentine • Theme from "New York, New York" • Over the Rainbow • Satin Doll • Some Day My Prince Will Come • Summertime • The Way You Look Tonight.

00103898 .... $9.99

THEME MUSIC

Mid-Intermediate Level

Batman Theme • Theme from E.T. (The Extra-Terrestrial) • Forrest Gump – Main Title (Feather Theme) • The Godfather (Love Theme) • Hawaii Five-O Theme • He's a Pirate • Linus and Lucy • Mission: Impossible Theme • Peter Gunn • The Pink Panther • Raiders March • (Ghost) Riders in the Sky (A Cowboy Legend) • Theme from Spider Man • Theme from "Star Trek®" • Theme from "Superman."

00103903 .... $9.99